Venture: The Risk is worthwhile

Elizabeth J. Hawks

Table of content

Chapter 1

Celesta, "Come on." Stella, a friend of mine, mumbled to me while blowing alcohol fumes in my face. Her lifeless arm was slung over my shoulder as I moaned. I supported Stella as she leaned on me, doing my best to prevent us both from falling. She was already drunk after only an hour of being here. I moved through the big, stench-filled house filled with alcohol and perfume. My nose was tickled by the pungent smell.

Where's Amelia? I asked my inebriated friend, but it was like speaking to a blank wall. Stella adjusted her gleaming green skirt for a brief while. Her beautiful blonde hair had become messy. To keep them from adhering to her blushing cheeks, I slid them behind her shoulder. The house was warm and muggy even though October had arrived.

She pointed to the dancing mob with a long finger and said, "Over there." Everyone looked greasy, and I instantly wrinkled my nose in disdain.

"I'll look after her," A chiseled football player named Milo arrived. Since their sophomore year, they had been dating. He swiftly combed his sandy brown hair back, then drew forward and ripped her arm away from me.

Oh, praise God. I sighed in relief as I gingerly took her off my shoulder. Stella laughed in response to her boyfriend's chuckle and encircled him in her arms.

Enjoy yourself, Celesta. Milo gave me a grin. I made an effort to give it back. Tonight, I felt incredibly sociopathic. My heart was heaving heavily.

"Celesta!" Over the loud music, Amelia called my name. I turned to see my red-cheeked pal bouncing about behind a few other individuals. She had been dancing the entire evening. Are you enjoying yourself? Amelia asked as she approached me and cast a troubled look my way.

I quickly nodded and said, "As much as I can." My lips came together in a tense grin. Amelia gave my hand a hard squeeze before holding it.

Come and dance. Before I could reprimand it, she pulled me in the direction of the group of people dancing.

Amelia enjoyed dancing. As she loved to remark, it's a part of our Mexican heritage.

I was being choked by the mixture of bodies rubbing up against me, the overpowering perfume, and the potent alcohol smell.

I saw my inebriated friend start to sway to the loud party music. The gorgeous blue outfit she was wearing highlighted her chocolate brown eyes, and her thick, black hair cascaded down her back. I initially awkwardly stood there, watching everyone else move their bodies to the music by dancing and swaying. Being that carefree must have felt good. I felt envious of them. I had a nasty tendency of overthinking things.

Dance Celesta, stop worrying about Philip," Amelia said, leaning in and placing her crimson lips near to my ear. When I heard his name, my heart began to hurt right away. Though I was aware that it was unavoidable, I never wanted to hear that name again.

I had entered my boyfriend's home three weeks earlier under the impression that we were going on a date. Instead, when I arrived, I saw him making out with another female in his room. He spoke some cruel remarks after I shouted at him, and I left. After everything was finished, I stopped talking to him. Three painful weeks have passed.

But Amelia was correct. Without her and Stella, I probably would still be a wreck as I hadn't left my room in an entire week.

Amelia shrieked loudly as another well-known song started playing, making me giggle at her response. I started to sway softly to the music, ignoring any ideas that were running through my head. My adrenaline level rose as I started to feel more at ease. It was good to finally have some respite. My mind was at rest for the first time in weeks as the rush of freedom took me. With my two closest buddies, I was out. All I needed was that.

Thankfully, I started to feel a little less tense once the song ended. "I'll go grab us some water," she said. I yelled above the loud music. Amelia nodded and kept dancing. That girl was capable of dancing all night long.

I was so hot that I was in dire need of a drink to quench my parched mouth. The unrelenting heat made my once-straight hair a frizzy disaster. I wanted to dive headfirst into a lake of ice. I hurriedly looked in the mirror, trembling at the sight of my red face.

When I entered the kitchen, there was a big queue of people attempting to get through.

It was packed in the little kitchen. I stood at the end of the line and puffed in irritation. More folks arrived and gathered behind me.

I looked around the busy space at the faces while I waited in line. My muscles tensed as soon as I caught sight of the familiar green eyes coming my way. My throat tightened as my heart jumped. Being taken by surprise made me feel exposed. I attempted to contain the flood of emotions that were flooding through me as panic overcame me.

"Go away from me." After yelling at Philip and sprinting away from the line, I lost my temper. I needed to get away from him as quickly as I could. As I looked around for one of my pals, my heart was racing. I was beginning to feel a lot of different feelings, and I was fighting back tears. This cannot be taking place. I wasn't yet ready to confront him, let alone this suddenly.

"Wait!" Philip called out to me. I scowled at the idea of having to speak with him. I wouldn't know what to say or do if it happened. Although they weren't as powerful as they had been, my feelings for him were still present.

I thought I was getting away from him pretty quickly, but a firm hand grabbed my elbow and threw me around, stopping me. I grind my teeth in annoyance.

I beg you not to flee. Philip pleaded while looking down at me. I clenched my hands into fists as I tried to recall all of my feelings. I was unable to express to him how big of an impact he made on me. My knuckles started to turn white from the tightness of my hold. Philip was slightly nudged from behind by a passerby before I could rip into him.

"Be careful." While glaring over his shoulder at me with green eyes, Philip hissed. I made every effort to escape from his hold, but I was unable. Still, we were too close to one another. My emotional state was not being helped by this.

"Pardon me?" The deep voice abruptly reverted. Philip turned to face the person behind him after breaking eye contact with me. I wasn't interested in waiting around to see what would transpire.

"You're the one who ran into me," she said. Philip snapped while attempting to sound intimidating. He released his hold on my elbow. I seized the chance to leave once more, but as I turned, he grasped my wrist firmly, inflicting a sharp pain that made me yell.

I turned around and saw Philip chatting to someone. Naturally, it was none other than George Kade. He had unruly blond hair, and when his intensely blue eyes met mine, it gave me the chills.

Do you treat your girlfriend like that?" George pointed at Philip's strangling hold on me. My entire body tensed up. The thought of Philip becoming my boyfriend once more nearly made me throw up. The words

George spoke made me furious all over. It just served to remind me of what had occurred, and I yanked my hand free from Philip's firm hold.

"I'm not dating him," she said. I spat angrily. I started to take deep breaths to control my escalating wrath as I could feel my blood starting to boil.

Philip blinked anguish in his green eyes as he turned to look at me in shock, but it was swiftly replaced by sternness.

You remain my girlfriend, I said. He moved toward me while pounding his teeth to emphasize the phrase.

I felt scared. Philip was showing his real colors. "I'm not your girlfriend," I said. My brain was swimming in the whole thing. I didn't want to experience these unfavorable feelings. Philip cheated on me, used foul language on me, and then wanted me to start talking to him again after a week or more. That could never have happened. I've come to understand that I merit much more.

I again winced as Philip firmly gripped my arm. I was being pierced by large fingers, and the pain forced me to firmly close my eyes. Never before have I been so afraid of him, let alone after seeing this side.

Why are you doing that? George hissed. You are doing her harm.

Keep your affairs in mind. To talk with George, Philip moved his head to his side. As soon as a few onlookers started to gather around the two agitated males, I wanted to vanish. My skin began to boil with shame as a small crowd started to gather.

"I'm not just going to sit here and watch you touch a female," she said. To stop Philip, George snapped and reached for his arm. Philip whirled around and made a fist at once.

George grinned inanely and avoided the swing with ease. Philip released me as he lunged at him while growling. Everyone turned to look at them as they both thudded loudly to the ground as they fell backward.

Within a second, George was back up and watching over Philip. Get up." Philip received a hard kick to the side when he snapped. He muttered something. "You can attempt to put your hands on me if you can get your hands on a female."

Philip stood up and punched George one more as his eyes grew gloomy. This time, George twisted his arm after grabbing it. As his arm was yanked from behind him, Philip yelped, but his scream was cut short by a loud snap that reverberated throughout the space. Philip's eyes rolled to the back of his head, and I gasped in amazement as I saw him fall to the ground.

My ex-boyfriend had just been knocked to the ground by George Kade.

Chapter 2

I STARED WITH WIDE EYES AT Philip's corpse as shock seeped into my bones. I was hardly able to grasp everything since everything happened so rapidly. I hadn't anticipated this to happen, and my fun-filled night was finished. My ex-boyfriend was now laying on the floor with a noticeable mark developing on the left side of his face since drama had taken control.

Amelia approached me quickly and exhaled as she saw Philip's lifeless body. "Holy crap. What took place?" Having wide eyes, she enquired. I looked up to see George fixating on me intensely with his bright electric blue eyes. They were hypnotizing, and I had the impression that he could read my mind.

"I'm grateful," I swallowed the lump in my throat back since my throat was dry, which helped a little bit.

"Celesta?" I was jolted out of my reverie by Amelia calling my name once more. I took a deep breath as I tore my gaze from George's. Philip was picked up by one of his pals and dragged toward the living room.

"Philip became quite physical." I made an effort to speak quietly so that only Amelia could hear me explain. By this time, a sizable throng had gathered around the incident. They were chatting quietly while gazing in astonishment at George.

They were treating him like a deity, and I found that to be annoying. I was aware that Philip deserved it, but not severely. He was unresponsive, and I wouldn't be shocked if his jaw had been broken. I sighed to myself as the obnoxious sound kept playing in my head.

When I told Amelia what I had, she gasped. "Are you alright? Has he injured you?"

Her anxious expression abruptly turned hostile. That jerk deserves it, I say. She continued, and I wholeheartedly concur. Even still, there was a part of me that was opposed to it. The only thing that may potentially make me blind is my feelings.

When I realized what she was asking, my head began to shake. "I'm good. Just a little shaken." I never anticipated seeing Philip here. I had hoped to have evaded him for a great deal longer.

He has always kept his distance from me, but I occasionally saw him at school. I questioned his purpose for being there. We spent a lot of our time together watching movies or catching up on our favorite TV episodes because Philip didn't like going to parties.

"Can you leave now that you've made a pointless scene?" George's sapphire eyes were fixed on me as I suddenly sprang up. Fortunately, I wasn't completely mesmerized by his gaze since his focus was so strong that I nearly instantly complied with him.

"I made a fuss?" I laughed incredulously. The altercation had been started by George!

"You, yes." The haughty youngster responded, sounding rather irritated. I kept his gaze, letting him know that I wasn't about to submit that quickly. I didn't even want to encounter Philip, to be honest. George's attitude was only making me feel angrier and more irritated than I already did.

"I just made a scene, and you just struck someone in the face?" I sounded slightly more enraged by raising my voice.

"Well, you're the one who brought him here, and I don't like naysayers. In addition, I have complete freedom. This celebration is mine." My cheeks turned red with shame as my heart stopped pounding in my chest. I didn't want anyone to believe that I was equally awful as Philip.

Out of everything I could have done tonight, I had to run into George and Philip, who was also hosting the event. All of the remaining bravery I had was wiped away by this one tiny, obvious truth, but I wasn't going to quit. I had no idea why Philip had done what he had, but I didn't want to be linked with him.

So, rather than explaining myself and making myself appear weak, I let my stress and rage take over.

"I don't mind. Jackson, get off your high horse. You are the source of the commotion." I snapped, releasing the wrath that had been building up inside of me. All of my feelings for Philip were now directed towards George.

George's eyes grew steely, and he moved closer to me. "It's

George," he said, crossing his arms to be formidable.

It was successful.

People started murmuring to themselves. "George intends to embarrass her. I feel sorry for her "Someone in the enquiring crowd mumbled. When I heard the remark, my teeth tightened. They were mistaken if they believed I cared about anything George said.

"I don't mind. I can immediately tell you're an

egotistical jerk who likes to push others about and thinks he's superior to everyone else." I snapped before storming past him and through the door.

The household waited for George to take some form of offense, but nothing materialized. I wasn't even aware that the music had been halted. I'm leaving because I want to, too. I continued as I left the comfortable home. A chilly breeze swirled my dark hair around my face as it approached. Amelia, trembling from the cold, caught up to me.

"I'm sure you're aware of what you have just done.

I'm not thinking clearly at the moment. I muttered as I made my way to Amelia's vehicle. I just wanted to go home and collapse into my luxurious bed.

George won't allow you to get away with this, he says. Amelia spoke while experiencing terror. She didn't improve my mood at all; on the contrary, she made it worse. All the drama and gossip throughout high school were its worst aspect. I couldn't help but be curious about what might transpire. Fortunately, I was in my senior year. There is just one more year to go.

"I know," I responded in a whisper, ignoring the chaotic thoughts running through my head.

While driving home, I sat in the car and deliberated about

my next move. I was so upset at Philip that I had let it out on George even though I knew I ought to have kept my mouth shut.

He deserved to be reprimanded, so at least I did. He pushed Philip out of the way for me, which I appreciated. Without George's intervention, I'm not sure what would have occurred.

It was going to be a long day on Monday.

Chapter 3

THE MONDAY AFTER, I had an anxious stomach ache as I entered school.

I attended two lessons with George. English and exercise. We had a few classes in common, so I had hoped to avoid seeing him for the coming week, but I knew that was impossible. There was no getting out of what I had done, and I now had to face the consequences.

I hurriedly entered English to sit as far away from him as possible.

While the majority of my classrooms had allocated seats, my English instructor was kind and let us choose where to sit.

As soon as I got there, I sat down in my normal chair. Which, given that it was so far in front, I concluded, was the best. As I proceeded to sit down, my backpack fell next to me with a loud bang, and someone yelled at me from behind.

A few while afterward, something bright hit the back of my skull. My entire body became rigid. And what was that? I looked down at the floor and saw the torn piece of paper.

I looked around the room, catching everyone's eyes. Not in front of everyone, I could not allow it to affect me. I was overcome with rage, but I was too determined to let it show, so I feigned to be unaffected. Naturally, George Kade was seated towards the rear of the classroom with a beaming smile on his face as I turned to glance around the room. I clench my teeth and resist the want to strike out at him immediately away.

Is this because Jackson thought I was an idiot, you ask? I made fun of him, anticipating that calling him by the incorrect name would enrage him once again. His smirk was somewhat reduced when it worked, but it was just enough for me to notice.

"George." The now-angry child corrected himself while gritting his teeth, confirming my assertion. I was frozen in place by George's narrowed, intensely blue eyes.

It was contentious eye contact. I stood up to go to the nurse's after my eyes started to tear away. As I left the room to go pretend to have a stomach ailment, the space was silent.

Amelia attempted to drink some water while she spoke, almost spitting it out all over me. I informed her of what had occurred earlier. After the nurses realized what had happened, I went back to the classroom, and everything was as normal as before.

"Don't worry about it given all that's occurred with Philip." I sighed in response to Amelia's hushed voice.

I find it unbelievable that he believed we were still dating. As I reached into my locker to transfer textbooks, my eyes met Amelia's. When something hairy moved close to it, my hand froze. It seemed strange. In my locker, I only had textbooks that were too heavy for me to talk about.

I started to draw my hand back but stopped as the anger thing moved once again, proving that it wasn't in my head. As my body froze, my heart began to pound erratically. I could feel my face tense up as my eyes were tightly closed. I squeaked as the object slid across the back of my hand.

What's on my hand, Amelia? As soon as I heard her gasp loudly, I was frozen with terror. That didn't bode well.

Don't let your eyes open. Amelia said in a trembling voice, "And don't move too quickly." She added apprehensively. While I had a curious side, I was frightened to find out. Whatever was on the back of my hand started to move once again and moved slowly toward my wrist. I thought I could hear my bones rattling because I was trembling so badly.

I snapped my eyes open out of sheer curiosity. I let out a scream when I noticed a large tarantula slithering across the back of my hand. Its furious legs kept creeping slowly past my wrist. I frantically waved my palm at it to get it away from me.

"Amelia! SLAY IT! Oh my God!" As I watched it slither inside my locker, I screamed. I'm terrified of spiders. I would cry every time I saw one. Not this time, though. I had no doubts whatsoever that George was responsible. He was pushing my limits despite my best efforts to keep him from getting to me.

From behind me, down the hallway, laughter broke out.

George was grinning broadly when I turned on my heels to look down the hallway. I was in a rage.

"You." I spat at him and stormed with hard feet at George. He attempted meekly to maintain his composure as I drew near...

When that failed, he attempted to suppress his laughter by covering his mouth with his palm while feigning a cough.

The joy in George's sparkling blue eyes was contagious. I note that you have met Spike.

I don't understand what you're attempting to achieve. To appear threatening, my palm brushed across his shoulder. "But I'm starting to feel pissed off," I said. I snarled and turned to go.

"I'm rather certain that item is a possession of Mr. Lopez's science class." As we rounded the corner into the following hallway, Amelia trembled. My head was smacked in the back by a little object. I performed a complete 180-degree turn with my body and was ready to choke George. Rather, I discovered a head poking out of a classroom. My stiff body relaxed, and I raised an incomprehensible eyebrow.

Come on, Celesta. The framed visage said, "Just you, though," in a low voice. He soon added. I ignored the familiar boy and shook my head as I started to turn. I can aid in your revenge on George. I paused mid-turn and gave Mario one more look. "Come here if you want my assistance." Amelia caught my eye as she nodded and moved on to her next lesson.

How specifically can you assist me? The boy with black hair who had just flinched openly at the door, I questioned.

I have something you can use to your advantage against him. In our history class on Friday, I'll leave it on your desk.
You must bring the items I am providing you to room B102

once you have them. All I need to know is where you are sitting." He went into great detail. The kind of instructions he was giving me made me feel as though I was about to go on a mission to save the planet. I quickly informed him of my seat assignment, but then I realized the question I had been itching to ask was beginning to come up.

Why are you assisting me? I cast a tight glare his way. I didn't even speak to this person, yet he decided to help me. I experienced a sense of being misled. I wasn't going to put up with anyone else in this school mistreating me any longer.

"Not for you, I assure you. Let's just say that George and I enjoy playing practical jokes on each other a lot, therefore I want him back. It so happens that it benefits you as well. You don't have to believe me right now, but you will on Friday. I'll see you then. Mario grinned at me briefly before returning to the lecture.

My eyes temporarily closed. You can complete this. After only one more day, we can depart for the weekend. As I made my way to my final class with Amelia, she smiled at me encouragingly.

Fortunately, this was the most tranquil of all days. Most people just wanted to go home and unwind because it was Friday.

The entire week had been a nightmare and had left me exhausted. I suffered quite a bit, but I made it. I avoided Philip for the majority of the week, although it was challenging because we had a few classes.

When I rounded the corner and saw George hanging out in the corridor with a few of his buddies, I couldn't help but grin. He grinned back and gave me the same wide-eyed look. He winked at me, and I rolled my eyes. He was mostly unaware of what would transpire. I wish I could have been there to witness his response. At least I had a chance of getting him back, even though I'm sure it was going to be priceless.

Earlier in history class, Mario gave me the assistance I required. He had shown me a photo of George from middle school when he had a quite different appearance. George's blond hair was cut in an ungainly bowl shape, and the eyeglasses he wore covered half of his acne-ridden face, giving the appearance that his eyes were considerably bigger than they were. Mario thought it was fair to publish the image, considering that George's last trick had gotten Mario suspended for two weeks, even though George reportedly despised it more than anything in the world. Mario didn't say what it was, but I went to the press department at the school and gave them the photo nevertheless.

The sixth period came around fast, and I waited patiently until the end of the lesson. The moment the TV in the room came on, I leaped in shock. Everyone turned their heads to the TV, expecting to see the school's news crew, but to their astonishment, something else was on. The moment the humiliating photo of George appeared, I refrained from laughing. Students conversed in whispers. I could not help but smile slyly.

Everyone left class as soon as the bell rang to enjoy their weekend. I immediately walked up to Amelia's locker and grinned furiously. I was eager to tell her everything. "From the insane expression on your face, something tells me you were engaged with what just transpired," Amelia said as she cast a glance my way.

I shook my head and grinned slyly at her. "Maybe."

Amelia was about to respond when her eyes widened and turned to look behind me. "This is where karma bites you in the behind." I looked back to see George approaching me ferociously. How could he know it was me already?

I ignored the uneasy knot rising in the pit of my stomach and bit my lip to keep from laughing. As George sped through, some innocent onlookers were pushed over, and they took a few steps back while staring at him. Knowing they shouldn't speak, they swore at him inaudibly as he passed.

How did you obtain the image? When he got to me, George snarled. I debated whether to just play a practical joke on him or deny that it was me. Of course, I go with option two.

What about Mario? I was unable to answer as George glared while he grunted. I was about to respond with a humorous rejoinder, but then a more devious thought occurred to me. Leaning closer until our faces were only a few inches apart, I cautiously placed both of my hands on his chest.

Is Jackson upset that he is losing? When our faces were just a few inches apart, I whispered. He was breathing more, so my plan was working. When I ran my fingertips down George's strong stomach, he sighed a little. Oh wow.

I drew back and chuckled icily, jolting him out of his reverie. I swung around to find a perplexed Amelia. "Let's leave." George stopped me by putting his hands firmly around my waist, which made me tighten up.

A strong chest dragged my body back against it. The left side of my neck was being rubbed by warm breathing, which made my skin shiver. His mouth went close to my ear while his eyes drifted shut.

"Don't try to win a game you can't."

Before his body heat vanished, George muttered. I relaxed before I opened my eyes. For me, this was just too intense. Even though George was obnoxious, I had to agree that he was gorgeous. Yet highly appealing while being frustrating.

"What occurred just now?" Wide-eyed, Amelia's brown eyes darted between George's back and my bewildered face. I mentally went over what had happened for a time before sighing in frustration. That didn't turn out as I had hoped, and it worked against me. I ought to have been wiser.

I believe I have gotten myself into some serious trouble.

www.ingramcontent.com/pod-product-compliance
Lightning Source LLC
LaVergne TN
LVHW052056160826
845678LV00015B/3257

* 9 7 9 8 8 4 6 9 5 1 2 9 7 *